To: _____

From: _____

Date: _____

WHAT WOULD JESUS DO SERIES

Ciana Publishers is dedicated to changing lives through books. Children will be empowered through the "What Would Jesus Do Series". Through these books, we spread the Good News of Jesus Christ, the hope of glory.
SJvR & LS

Copyright © 2024 by Sybrand JvR & Lucia S.
All rights reserved. Published by Ciana Publishers

This Book is Copyright Protected:
This is only for personal use. You cannot amend, distribute, sell, use, quote, or paraphrase any part of the content within this book without the consent of the author. The Author guarantees all contents are original and do not infringe upon the legal rights of any other person or work.

No part of this book may be reproduced, duplicated, or transmitted in any form by means such as printing, scanning, photocopying, or otherwise, without direct written permission from the author or publisher, except for the use of quotations in a book review
and as permitted by the U.S. copyright law.
For permission, contact info@cianapublishers.com.

Disclaimer and Terms of Use:
This book is provided solely for entertainment, motivational and informational purposes.

All Scripture quotations, unless otherwise indicated, are taken from the Holy Bible, New International Version®, NIV®. Copyright ©1973, 1978, 1984, 2011 by Biblica, Inc.TM Used by permission of Zondervan. All rights reserved worldwide. www.zondervan.comThe "NIV" and "New International Version" are trademarks registered in the United States Patent and Trademark Office by Biblica, Inc.TM

Authors – Sybrand JvR & Lucia S

2nd Edition 2024

www.cianapublishers.com

CHARACTER DESCRIPTIONS

Ji-hoon

Ji-hoon mostly dwells in his own world, being a perfectionist and introverted genius who is exceptionally loyal.
He loves playing chess, and his dream is to become a great mathematician. He is well-read and speaks with wisdom.
He is calm, calculated, and very protective and acts like Elsa's big brother. He loves Jesus a lot and this love overflows to others.

Elsa

Elsa is a bubbly, self-assured go-getter who isn't afraid to speak her mind and she is quick to act. Her strengths are that she is bold, confident, and fearless. She loves to dance, play drums, and play sports. She is always looking for adventure.
As a spontaneous ball of happiness, when she's around, excitement is sure to follow. Her favourite Bible character is Esther, who made a big difference in her surroundings.

Rheya

Rheya is a brilliant little chef, and she loves reading. She is very caring, and she makes time for everyone. Her challenges have taught her to appreciate life. She has a positive attitude and is a clever girl who gets top marks in all her subjects.

Oliver

Oliver is a wrestler who loves hotdogs and switch games. He loves using the word 'dude'. He uses the word so much that his nickname is Dude. He loves to spread stories. Where there is an argument, Oliver is there to join in and cause confusion and trouble.

Gina

Gina loves hockey and is very good at it. She is popular and easily influences those around her. She is getting herself in a lot of trouble for not thinking before she speaks. She spreads stories without confirming whether they are true. She seeks confrontations and is always angry and proud.

Mrs Harris

Mrs Harris is back. She has a kind heart and a listening ear. She gives good advice. She is strict and demands good discipline and respect for each other. Mrs Harris is very caring and is always ready to go the extra mile.

HAVE YOU EVER... DID YOU EVER...

Have you ever joined others to gossip about something that wasn't true?

Did you ever go out of your way to find out the truth?

Have you ever made up lies about someone else?

Did you ever hear something and later realise you heard wrong?

Do you know you can ask Jesus about the truth when you aren't sure?

Little did Ji-hoon and Elsa know that their characters would be tested over the next few days. The question is, will they pass the test?

Wanna see how Ji-hoon and Elsa went about finding out the truth?

Let's dive in and find out.

 Samantha, you are fourth. Jody, you are third.
Good job, girls.
Jody, your hard work is paying off.

 Well done, Samantha. Well done, Jody.

 Well done, Ji-hoon for taking second place.
Outstanding job, Rheya, in her absence,
on securing first place.

 What, second! Impossible!

 Ji-hoon, you will smash it next time.

 How could this…? Rheya doesn't even come to class. I work hard and never miss a class.

 You are second; chill!

 I'm always first. I don't understand. Something isn't quite right!

 Ji-hoon, I agree. Something is wrong.

 Something's OFF dude! When was the last time you guys saw Rheya at school?

 Well, I saw Mrs Harris walking with Rheya the other day. In fact, I saw Mrs Harris walking with Rheya a few times!

 Gina, Oliver, REALLY!

 Dude, something isn't right. You are never second.

 I know, right? See Elsa! What others think of me is on the line.

 Chill! You mean your reputation. I learned this word last week. Am I not smart, or what?

 This is no time for jokes.

Please, Elsa, don't try to be clever here.

 Ji-hoon you take all of this WAY too seriously.

 This is serious!
Rheya probably gets the questions and answers.

 Hmm. All I know is that something isn't quite right.

 I told you guys that SOMETHING IS OFF!

 STOP! You don't know what is really going on.

 Mrs Harris will never do such a thing. Who says it wasn't just pure hard work?

 Kids! Are you done talking? I would like to continue with the lesson.

This isn't fair!

Oliver, do you want to share something with the class?

No Ma'am.

SCHOOL CANTEEN

 Hey Ji-hoon! Over here, dude.
We need to talk about this whole 'Rheya thing'.

 Yes, let us discuss the matter at hand.
Come, Elsa, let's join them.

 No! Ji-hoon, I'm not interested!

 Why are you like this?

 Do you actually believe all this?

 N-no. I mean, I don't... but it's worth investigating.

 Hmm, I wonder? You don't sound very convinced. We've gotta be careful about jumping on board with stuff when there's no proof, you know?

THE NEXT DAY...

 Good morning, class.
Take your seats and take out your books.

 Mrs Harris gives Rheya
the test questions beforehand.

 Exactly, and that isn't all;
she gets the answers too.

 STOP THIS nonsense!

SCHOOL CANTEEN

 Hey! Are you guys joining us today? Sit down.

 Welcome to the 'table of investigation'. We are onto something BIG.

I have to hear this.

I don't have time for this. I'm leaving.

 Go and sit at another table. You are so boring.

 Looking for the truth isn't boring; it's the right thing to do.

 We got our facts from reliable sources. We are standing up for what is right. This is doing the right thing.

Well, you and Oliver are going by hearsay. Goodbye!!!

OUTSIDE THE PRINCIPAL'S OFFICE

- Sir... Rheya's mark... The school... Mom... money....

- OH MY WORD! This is shocking!

- Did you hear that? NO WAY, dude!

- Rheya gets better marks because her mom has paid money to the school. Can you even believe your ears?

 Dude and I are going to follow Mrs Harris.

 Blah-blah! Ever thought gossiping could backfire like a boomerang?

 Shh! Don't waste your breath.

 Hmm… Just thinking… 'A Gina Gossip Hour.' Wonder how you'd like being the star?

SHAPING TOMORROW'S LEADERS

RHEYA'S HOUSE

 Elsa, you gave me such a fright. I thought you were going to Rheya's house.

 THIS IS Rheya's house!

 Oh, my golly penguin! I didn't know that this was Rheya's house. So, it's true!

 Shuu! Be Quiet!

I am homeschooling for a bit until my mom gets better.

Your mom is so blessed to have a daughter like you. You work hard and take such good care of her.

The principal and teachers have been helping us with food and money, too.

We thank God for everything. God is so good.

THE NEXT DAY...

 Good morning, class. Some of you are spreading rumours without knowing what is really going on.

We know what is happening, Ma'am.

You were exposed! We know everything.

 Gina! Oliver! You should be ashamed of yourselves! Go and confirm your facts at the principal's office. RIGHT NOW! Wait for me there!

 Class, let us keep Rheya and her mom in our thoughts and prayers.

 Ma'am, I am very sorry. I felt jealous because Rheya beat me in maths.

 It's in the past now, Ji-hoon. All is well. Class, let us always confirm our facts before we spread rumours.

 Ma'am, Ruby and I will go and visit Rheya more often.

 When you guys go, I will take my science set and discuss maths formulas. Rheya is so smart.

 ARGH NO! Maths and science again?

HaHaHa!!!

WHAT WOULD JESUS DO?

 Once again my grandfather was proved right - don't rush to judge people by what you hear or see.

 Elsa, you are a Nicodemus of our time.
You couldn't be swayed by Gina and Oliver.

 Thanks, Ji-hoon! Oh wow, please say more.

 You didn't jump to conclusions. You were determined to discover the truth. Nowadays, people lack the patience to search for the truth.

 Ahh, thank you! SO TRUE! We want everything instantly! Like, we can munch on something in less than two minutes. And zip, a message flies across the world in just a sec.

 Nicodemus didn't sit around and listen to what others had to say about Jesus. He had an independent mind.

 AN INDEPENDENT MIND?
What's that?

 An independent mind thinks for itself.
It's a mind that's ready to find out the truth.

 Grandpa Nico showed a hunger to learn from Jesus.

 Absolutely! He showed this by visiting Jesus by night in search of the truth.

 Shame, it wasn't easy for Grandpa Nico. His friends gossiped about Jesus.

 Thank God he didn't join the gossipers. Secondly, as Israel's teacher, he wasn't intimidated by Jesus, who performed great signs and wonders. Instead, he was ready to learn from Him.

 I'm glad everyone now knows the truth about Rheya. She's so sweet.

 She is focused and smart. I was proud and didn't want to accept defeat.

 You totally rocked it by owning up and saying sorry. I'm super proud of you!

 I know that Jesus used these few days to humble me so that I could be reminded that ALL IS OF GRACE.

LET'S PRAY

Father, may Your Spirit who dwells in my heart be the voice of my prayer, in Jesus' name.

Jesus help me to have a heart that is rooted in Your Word and a heart that is ready to find out the truth.

Lord, Jesus, fill me with Your love until it overflows to others.

In Jesus' name.

Amen.

BIBLE VERSES TO CHECK OUT

John 3:1-16, Romans 12:1-2, Proverbs 26:20, 1 Corinthians 13:1-7,

Matthew 22:37-39, John 19:38-42

INSPIRATIONAL QUOTES

Instead of gossiping, find out the truth.

Proverbs 26:20, Ephesians 4:25, Titus 3:2

Be known for spreading truth, not lies.

Proverbs 12:22, 16:28, Colossians 3:9-10

A teaspoon of truth is enough to stop a truckload of lies.

Proverbs 26:20, John 8:32, 2 Corinthians 13:8

As fire dies out with water; gossip dies out with truth.

Leviticus 19:16, Proverbs 20:19, 26:20, Ephesians 4:29

A gossipmonger thrives on gossip; a champion thrives on truth.

Proverbs 11:13, 16:28, James 1:26

Going by hearsay is like getting into a vehicle, not knowing where it's going.

Proverbs 20:19, John 3:1-3, 8:32

LET'S CHAT

What can we learn from Ji-hoon? Mention two positive and two negative examples.
_____
_____
_____

Are you like Gina and Oliver, or do you have some 'Gina and Oliver' friends? What are those negative examples not to follow?
_____
_____
_____

When you hear rumours; how will you respond?
_____
_____
_____

What did you enjoy about this story? How does this story inspire you?
_____
_____
_____

What gave Nicodemus the courage to visit Jesus by night?
_____
_____
_____

What do you understand about having an independent mind?
_____
_____
_____

OTHER BOOKS IN
THE WHAT WOULD JESUS DO SERIES

  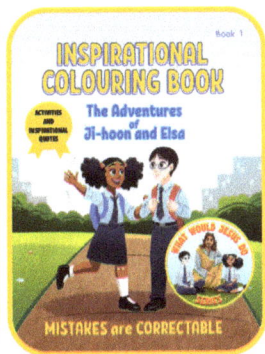  

OTHER BOOKS BY THE AUTHORS

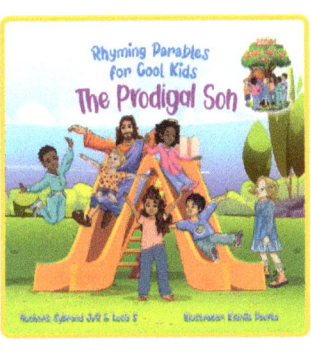